# Lamb of God

Key Biblical Messianic Prophecies

Pauline Shone

# Lamb of God

## Key Biblical Messianic Prophecies

Pauline Shone

LAMB OF GOD
Key Biblical Messianic Prophecies
ISBN: 978-0-9557729-4-8
Copyright © 2013, 2014 2025 by Pauline Shone (the author),
 Simon Books, Derbyshire, England.

All rights reserved. No part of this book may be reproduced, stored in a retrievable system, or transmitted in any way by any means—electronic, mechanical, photocopying, recording, or otherwise—without the prior written permission of the copyright holder, according to USA copyright law.

Published by
### *Olive Shoots*
an Imprint of:
**O**live Press Publisher
www.olivepressbooks.com
www.olivepresspublisher.com
olivepressbooks@gmail.com

\

Cover design and artwork by the author.
Printed in the USA and UK

Formerly published by:
 Zaccmedia (2013)
 Authentic Media, O.M. Books Foundation (2014)

**NOTE**: Having a British author and an American publisher, the choice was made to mainly use American grammar and spelling.

All Scriptures are taken from the *New King James Version*. Copyright © 1982 by Thomas Nelson, Inc. Used by permission. All rights reserved.

## DEDICATION

This book is dedicated to the memory of Derek and Lydia Prince. Lydia's true-life story, *Appointment in Jerusalem*, written by her husband Derek Prince, was instrumental in leading me to a personal faith in the Jewish Messiah.

Lydia's personal experiences and Derek's prophetic insights from Scripture were a valuable foundation on which to begin building an understanding of Israel. Events that take place in this tiny country are of worldwide significance.

# FOREWORD

"Pauline Shone has done a very good and creative job in collecting and briefly commenting on the key Messianic Biblical prophecies. I am sure this book, helpfully divided into fourteen chapters, will be a highly valued introductory resource in many evangelistic, teaching and devotional contexts. It is always encouraging to our understanding and our faith to see the unfolding of God's purposes throughout history, so clearly stated in Scripture. As the truths of Scripture are presented our thankfulness for the faithfulness of God in the past and present increases, also our hope and trust for the future is renewed."

**Rev Alex Jacob M.A, M.PHIL**
URC SYNOD MINISTER (MISSION PARTNERSHIPS)
Formerly, CEO, THE CHURCHES MINISTRY AMONG JEWS UK

"The *Lamb of God* outlines some of the major prophecies about the Messiah of Israel and Savior of the world, Jesus the Christ. This little book amplifies as well as clarifies the need for a sacrificial atonement for each individual. Anyone searching for truth can read and find the One who awaits those willing to accept the Lamb of God slain from the foundation of time. The Lamb is precious and so is this book."

**Sharon Sanders, Co-Founder,**
CHRISTIAN FRIENDS OF ISRAEL JERUSALEM

"Behold! The Lamb of God
who takes away the sin of the world!"
John 1:29

... redeemed ... with the precious blood
of Christ, as of a lamb
without blemish and without spot ...
before the foundation of the world....
I Peter 1:18-20

And I looked, and behold,
in the midst of the throne ...,
stood a Lamb
as though it had been slain....
Revelation 5:6

... the Lamb slain
from the foundation of the world.
Revelation 13:8

## CONTENTS

| | |
|---|---|
| Foreword | 6 |
| Introduction | 11 |
| 1. The First Prophecy Concerning Messiah | 13 |
| 2. Prophecies Concerning Messiah's Earthly Ancestry | 15 |
| 3. Prophecies Concerning a Forerunner | 26 |
| 4. Prophecies Concerning Messiah's Birth | 30 |
| 5. Prophecies Concerning Messiah's Birthplace | 33 |
| 6. Prophecies of Messiah's Pre-Existence | 38 |
| 7. Prophecies Concerning A Sacrificial Lamb | 41 |
| 8. Prophecies of Messiah's Earthly Ministry | 52 |
| 9. Prophecies of Messiah's Betrayal | 61 |
| 10. Prophecies of Messiah's Suffering | 67 |
| 11. Prophecies of Messiah's Death and Burial | 75 |
| 12. Prophecies of Messiah's Resurrection | 79 |
| 13. Prophecies of Messiah's Second Coming | 85 |
| 14. Prophecies of Messiah's Everlasting Kingdom | 94 |
| About the Author | 98 |
| Other Books by the Author | 100 |

# INTRODUCTION

The first ten chapters in this book follow a thread of key Messianic Biblical prophecies that foretell the coming of the Messiah. It also studies the events that exactly fulfilled these promises, recorded in the Bible and verified by reliable witnesses.

The last two chapters cover some of the future Biblical prophecies relating to Messiah's return, and their possible course of fulfillment.

Only God Himself knows the exact times and seasons of all the Biblical prophecies and complex events yet to take place. However, as they will all be fulfilled in Israel, it is very significant that Jewish people are back in the land of their forefathers.

## Chapter One

# The First Prophecy Concerning Messiah

## Seed Of A Woman

"And I will put enmity

Between you and the woman,

And between your seed and her Seed;

**He shall bruise your head,**

**And you shall bruise His heel.**"

Genesis 3:15, emphasis added

God had told Adam and Eve that they could eat freely from the fruit of every tree in the Garden of Eden. However, there was one exception. He warned them not to eat from the tree of the knowledge of good and evil that was in the middle of the garden. If they ate its fruit they would die.

## Chapter 1

Then one day the serpent came to Eve and introduced doubt about what God had clearly stated. Then he contradicted God's word, saying that they would not die if they ate the forbidden fruit. He also questioned God's motives for the restriction; saying that God knew their eyes would be opened when they ate this fruit, and they would become like God, knowing good and evil.

The temptation to ignore God's warning and disobey Him was initiated by Satan; and listening to his cunning lies had led to a rebellion against God's commandment. Because of what he had done, God cursed the serpent. God also declared that there would be enmity between the serpent and the woman; and between his seed and the woman's Seed.

This was not just about snakes, it was indirectly about Satan, the enemy of our souls. And within this ambiguous language is a promise of a Child, the coming Messiah. He would eventually defeat the serpent's seed, but Satan would cause Him great suffering.

(Cont. Chapter 3 and 7)

## Chapter Two

# Prophecies Concerning Messiah's Earthly Ancestry

**Shem**

> "Blessed be the LORD,
>
> The God of Shem,
>
> And may Canaan be his servant.
>
> May God enlarge Japheth,
>
> And may he dwell in the tents of Shem;
>
> And may Canaan be his servant."
>
> Genesis 9:26-27

After the flood, when the earth had dried, God told Noah and his family to leave the ark and bring out all the living creatures with them. Then Noah built an altar to the LORD and made a burnt offering on it. His sacrifice was pleasing and acceptable to God. He promised that He would not curse the earth again, nor would He destroy every living thing.

## Chapter 2

God blessed Noah and his sons, Shem, Ham and Japheth. They became the fathers of three new nations, and this new populating of earth provided a fresh beginning for humankind.

Noah planted a vineyard and became drunk with the wine. While he lay uncovered in his tent, Ham, father of Canaan, looked at his father's nakedness. Then he went outside and told his brothers. But Shem and Japheth took a cloak, and walked backwards into the tent. Then with their faces turned away, they covered him.

When Noah woke up he knew what had happened to him. But he could not curse Ham for disrespecting him, as Noah and his sons had already been blessed by God. So he cursed Ham indirectly, by cursing his son Canaan (Genesis 9:25; Deuteronomy 27:16).

Then Noah blessed the LORD, the God of Shem, giving Shem precedence over his two brothers (Genesis 9:26-27). It was God's plan that the Messiah would come from the descendants of Shem and be a member of the Semitic race.

## Abraham

> "I will make you a great nation;
>
> I will bless you
>
> And make your name great;
>
> And you shall be a blessing.

I will bless those who bless you,

And I will curse him who curses you;

And in you all the families of the earth

shall be blessed."

Genesis 12:2-3

God commanded Abram, a descendant of Shem, to leave his country, his family, and his tribe for a land that He would show him. God blessed Abram and promised that he would become the father of a great nation, a people belonging to God. Later, God changed Abram's name to Abraham, meaning father of nations. He is also the father of Ishmael and his descendants, as well as people groups descended from children borne to him by Keturah, his wife after Sarah had died.

It was God's sovereign choice that His people would live in the land of Canaan, later renamed Israel. And it was God's foreordained plan that Messiah would be born there; and as a descendant of the family line of Judah, that He would be a Jew.

Abraham, and his descendants were commanded to be a blessing to all peoples. And through them came the Holy Spirit inspired written Scriptures, God's Laws, the Biblical prophets, the Messiah, the apostles, and the Gospel of Good News.

## Chapter 2

## Isaac

> But God said to Abraham, "Do not let it be displeasing in your sight because of the lad or because of your bondwoman. Whatever Sarah has said to you, listen to her voice; for in Isaac your seed shall be called."
>
> Genesis 21:12 emphasis added

Abraham and Sarah had waited many years for the fulfillment of God's promise to give them a son. And as Sarah was well past the age of child bearing, she persuaded Abraham to sleep with her Egyptian handmaid, Hagar. (Using a surrogate mother to have children was an accepted custom). *But when Hagar became pregnant she despised her mistress. Therefore there was enmity between the two women* (Genesis 16:1-4).

At one time, both Abraham and Sarah had laughed at the idea of having a son in their old age (Genesis 17:17; 18:12). Yet at God's appointed time, Sarah miraculously conceived and gave birth to Isaac. And at ninety years of age, she was able to nurse (feed) her son!

Abraham gave a party the day that Isaac was weaned from breast milk. But during the celebration Sarah saw Ishmael mocking Isaac, and she insisted that Abraham cast out the slave woman and her son, saying that Ishmael would not be an heir with her son, Isaac!

Of course this troubled Abraham, who loved Ishmael. And God spoke to him directly, instructing him to listen to his wife. God said He would bless Ishmael and make him into a great nation. But it was His sovereign choice that the messianic line would continue through Isaac, the son of the promise.

## Jacob

> "I see Him, but not now;
> I behold Him, but not near;
> A Star shall come out of Jacob;
> A Scepter shall rise out of Israel,
> And batter the brow of Moab,
> And destroy all the sons of tumult."
>
> Numbers 24:17

Isaac's wife, Rebekah, was pregnant and her babies struggled together in the womb. So Rebekah asked the LORD what was happening. He told her that there were two nations in the womb. One people would be stronger than the other, and the older would serve the younger.

Esau was the first twin to be born, followed by Jacob, who came out grasping his brother's heel! Esau became a skillful hunter in the fields, whereas Jacob was a quiet indoors man.

One day, Esau returned home hungry and wanted some of the lentil stew that Jacob had cooked. Being an opportunist, Jacob asked for his brother's firstborn birthright in exchange.

Then exaggerating his hunger, Esau asked what use his birthright was if he was about to die? So he despised his birthright by selling it to Jacob for a bowl of lentil stew! Esau also married Hittite women, who believed in many gods, and this caused his parents great distress.

When Isaac was dying, Rebekah encouraged Jacob to deceive his father into giving him the firstborn's blessing.

## Chapter 2

And between them, they successfully tricked the nearly blind Isaac into believing Jacob was his brother, Esau. So Jacob received the firstborn's blessing, causing enmity between the brothers.

Fearing for her favorite son's life, Rebekah sent Jacob to her brother Laban in Haran. Yet, despite all the human scheming, it was God's will that His promises to Abraham and Isaac would be inherited by Jacob, and not by Esau, the firstborn.

## The Twelve Sons of Jacob

Reuben, Simeon, Levi, Judah, Dan, Naphtali, Gad, Asher, Issachar, Zebulan, Joseph, Benjamin.

Jacob loved Laban's younger daughter at first sight and offered to serve his uncle seven years in exchange for Rachel as his wife. However, although Laban had agreed to this, he said it was the custom for the eldest daughter to be married first.

So on Jacob's wedding night, Laban deliberately deceived his nephew and sent his eldest daughter, Leah, to him. Yet Jacob loved Rachel so much, that he was willing to work seven more years to marry her!

God blessed Leah, the unloved wife, with children; but Rachel was unable to conceive. Hence there was rivalry between the two women. Leah desired Jacob's love, and Rachel envied Leah's ability to conceive.

Over time, Leah had six sons, and a daughter. Rachel's maid, Bilhah, served as a surrogate mother for her mistress and bore two sons. Leah's maid, Zilpah, also served her mistress as a surrogate mother and she also bore two sons.

Then God enabled Rachel to conceive and she gave birth to Joseph. Later in life, Rachel would have a second son, Benjamin, but she died shortly after giving birth to him.

## Judah

"The Scepter shall not depart

from Judah,

Nor a lawgiver from between his feet,

Until Shiloh [*Messiah] comes;

And to Him shall be the obedience

of the people."

Genesis 49:10, *author's note

In his last days, Jacob gathered his twelve sons around him and spoke to them individually. Beginning with his firstborn Reuben, he declared what would happen to them in the future.

Jacob rebuked and demoted Reuben, Simeon and Levi's position in the family: Reuben because of his actions with Bilhah (Genesis 35:22); Simeon and Levi because of their excessively cruel revenge against Shechem and his people (Genesis: 34).

Jacob praised Judah greatly, saying that he was like a mighty lion, and his brothers would bow down before him. And in blessing Judah, Jacob predicted that a royal line would arise from his descendants and rule until Shiloh (Messiah) came.

## Chapter 2

In the seemingly haphazard chaos of individuals' flawed natures and family discord, God patiently and graciously continued working to fulfill His plan. The Messiah-King would come from the descendants of Jacob's son, Judah.

Jacob also blessed Joseph, the son betrayed by his brothers, yet strengthened through his trials. The Mighty God of Jacob had protected and blessed Joseph. Rachel's firstborn and Jacob's favorite had been separated to serve God's holy purposes.

### Jesse

> Of the increase
>
> of His government and peace
>
> There will be no end,
>
> Upon the throne of David
>
> and over His kingdom,
>
> To order it and establish it
>
> with judgment and justice
>
> From that time forward, even forever.
>
> The zeal of the LORD of hosts
>
> will perform this.
>
> Isaiah 9:7

**There shall come forth**

**a Rod from the stem of Jesse,**

**And a Branch shall grow out of his roots.**

Isaiah 11:1

Led by Joshua, the children of Israel invaded Canaan, conquered the people, and took possession of the land. Then each tribe (family) of Israel received a portion of the land as their inheritance.

Under the godly leadership of Joshua, the Israelites had been faithful to the God of Israel, and all went well. However after Joshua's death, Israel was led by judges, and the Israelites turned from God's laws. So everyone did what they considered to be right by their own standards.

For nearly four centuries there were repeated cycles of rebellion against God, leading to defeat by their enemies, and then repentance and a return to God.

Samuel was the last judge, and he was also a prophet. During his leadership, there was a transition from judges to kings. The Israelites no longer wanted God as King; they wanted to be like the other nations and have a man to reign over them.

Saul was anointed by Samuel to be the first king of Israel. But although his outward appearance was impressive, he did not follow the LORD wholeheartedly, or fully obey His commandments. God regretted that He had made Saul king, and He chose a young man after his heart to replace him.

CHAPTER 2

## David

God told Samuel to take anointing oil and go to Jesse the Bethlehemite because He had chosen a king from one of his sons. From the many tribes of Judah, God had chosen David, the youngest son of Jesse, to be the anointed king of Israel and an ancestor of Messiah, the Eternal King.

Saul had lost the blessing of God's presence, and he was jealous of David's anointing and popularity. Therefore he hated David as an enemy, and throughout the remainder of his reign he continually persecuted him. Although an anointed future king, David had to live as a fugitive and fight to survive. Yet he would not harm Saul, even when he had the opportunity to do so, (1 Samuel 24 and 26)

David was a charismatic leader and courageous warrior, gathering many followers to himself during his years of exile. The LORD sees what is inside a man, and He knew that David loved Him with all his heart.

After Saul was killed in a battle with the Philistines, the men of Judah anointed David to rule as king over them. David reigned in Hebron for seven and a half years. Then he was anointed king over all the tribes of Israel. From Jerusalem, David reigned over all Israel and Judah for thirty-three years.

## Fulfillment

Jews kept meticulous records, and all public registers were carefully preserved. There are two genealogies recorded in the Bible concerning Jesus' birth.

Matthew's Gospel records Jesus' genealogy from Abraham, Isaac, and Jacob; and he traces His legal inheritance line through David's son, Solomon.

Luke's Gospel records Jesus' genealogy from Joseph, all the way back to Adam; and His royal bloodline through Nathan, another of David's sons.

It could be that Matthew traced Joseph's ancestral line and Luke traced Mary's history. Joseph and Mary were most probably of the same tribe and family, according to the Jewish law (Numbers 36:8).

# Chapter Three

# Prophecies Concerning A Forerunner

The voice of one crying in the wilderness:

"Prepare the way of the LORD;

Make straight in the desert

A highway for our God."

Isaiah 40:3

"Behold, I send My messenger,

And he will prepare the way before Me.

And the Lord, whom you seek,

Will suddenly come to His temple,

Even the Messenger of the covenant,

In whom you delight.

Behold, He is coming,"

Says the LORD of hosts.

Malachi 3:1

Prophecies concerning a forerunner, who would precede the coming of Messiah and prepare His way were well known among Jews. After the time of the prophet Malachi, no other prophets had appeared in Israel. There was a period of silence lasting about 400 years. Then John the Baptist came as God's messenger to prepare the people of Israel for the coming of the promised Messiah.

## Priest Zacharias

From 37 B.C. to 4 B.C. Judea, Samaria, and Galilee were governed by Rome. Herod the Great, half Idumaean and half Israelite, was appointed under Roman patronage and ruled as king over Judea.

The Jews deeply resented the Roman occupation and hated the ruthlessly ambitious King Herod. Their only hope for liberation was centered on God's prophecies of a Messiah-King who would reign over Israel forever on the throne of David.

During the time that King Herod was ruling in Judea, there was a certain priest named Zacharias, of the division of Abijah. He and his wife were righteous Jews, who loved God and kept the requirements of His law. They had no children, as Elizabeth was barren, and they were both old.

When Zacharias's division was serving at the Temple in Jerusalem, he was chosen by lot to burn incense to the LORD. This was a great honor, something that a priest could only do once in his career.

At the hour that the incense was offered and the people were praying outside the Temple, Zacharias was startled by the sudden appearance of an angel, standing at the right side of the altar of incense.

## Chapter 3

The angel told him not to be afraid, his prayers had been heard. His wife would have a son and they were to name him John. He would be a prophet, consecrated to God and filled with the Holy Spirit from his mother's womb. He would go before Messiah in the spirit and power of Elijah to call people to repentance, and prepare them for the coming of the Lord.

But Zacharias looked at his natural circumstances and struggled to believe the angel's incredible pronouncement. Then the angel said that his name was Gabriel, and that he had been sent by God. And because Zacharias had doubted his message, he would be mute until God's promise was fulfilled.

### Witnesses: The Worshiping Crowd

The people waiting outside wondered why Zacharias was taking so long in the Temple. When he finally came out, he could not speak to them. Then they perceived that he had seen a vision.

### Witnesses: Neighbors And Friends

After Zacharias had completed his days of service at the Temple, he returned home. Later his wife conceived, and she withdrew for the first five months of her pregnancy. When it was time for her to give birth, she had a son. On the eight day they came to circumcise him, and everyone expected the baby to be named Zacharias after his father. But Elizabeth said that his name was John.

Her relatives and neighbors were surprised, as it was customary to name a child after a relative, and no one in the family had that name. Zacharias was deaf and mute, so they used sign language to ask him what name he would like to give his son. So Zacharias took a writing tablet and wrote, "His name is John."

Immediately Zacharias was able to speak again and began praising God. Everyone living in the hill country of Judea was filled with awe at these events and wondered what this child would become, for surely the hand of the LORD was upon him!

Zacharias, filled with the Holy Spirit, prophesied. He said that the God of Israel was fulfilling His promises made through the prophets down the ages to send the Saviour, a descendant of David, to Israel. And John would prepare the way before Him by informing the people of their need to repent of their sins and receive forgiveness.

## Fulfillment

John grew up, became strong in spirit, and lived in the desert until it was time for him to preach to Israel.

(Cont. Chapter 7)

## Chapter Four

# Prophecies Concerning Messiah's Birth

### Immanuel

> "Therefore the Lord Himself shall give you a sign: Behold, the virgin shall conceive and bear a Son, and shall call His name Immanuel."     Isaiah 7:14

God promised this sign to king Ahaz of the house of David. This prophecy says that a virgin will conceive and give birth to a Son — a miracle. And His name will be Emmanuel (which means 'God is with us').

Revelation 12:1-6 speaks of this great sign, and the spiritual opposition that would war against this male Child, the Jewish Messiah. The spiritual battle would also be against the Jewish nation and all Messiah's followers. (See the Daniel 9:20-27 prophecy.)

A woman conceiving without a man is a biological impossibility. But as God created the heavens and the earth, and man from the dust of the earth, He could certainly bring about a virgin birth.

## Fulfillment

Six months after Elizabeth's conception, God sent the angel Gabriel to a virgin named Mary, living in the city of Nazareth in Galilee. Entering her home, Gabriel greeted Mary and told her to rejoice, for she was highly favored, the LORD was with her, and she was blessed among women.

Mary was shaken by the angel's visitation and confused by his greeting. But the angelic visitor reassured Mary, saying that he had come with a message from God.

Mary would conceive and give birth to a Son. His name would be Jesus. He would be great and called the Son of God. The LORD God would give Him the throne of His ancestor David, and He would rule over Jacob's house forever. Mary believed the message, but struggled to comprehend how it could be accomplished. So Gabriel explained that the Holy Spirit would come upon her and she would conceive by the power of God.

Then Gabriel told Mary that her relative Elizabeth had conceived a son, even though she was old and everyone had thought she was barren. She was now six months pregnant. Mary knew that her reputation would be at stake, but she asked no questions and humbly surrendered to the plan and purpose of God.

## Witnesses: Elizabeth and John

Soon after this experience, Mary visited her cousin Elizabeth. At the sound of her greeting, Elizabeth's baby jumped for joy, and she was filled with the Holy Spirit. So

## Chapter 4

before Mary could share her news, Elizabeth already knew that she had been chosen to be the mother of the Lord.

Elizabeth declared that Mary was blessed among women, and the fruit of her womb was blessed. She marveled at the privilege of Mary's visit, saying that those things promised to her would come to pass because she had believed.

### Witness: Joseph

Now Mary was engaged to Joseph, a direct descendant of King David. When he discovered that Mary was pregnant, it appeared that she had betrayed him. Bitterly disappointed, he wanted to break off the engagement. But being a good man, a devout Jew, he desired to do it discreetly; so that Mary would not be shamed and disgraced.

While Joseph was grappling with this dilemma, God's angel spoke to him in a dream, telling him to marry Mary, as the Baby conceived in her was from the Holy Spirit. She would have a Son and He was to be named Jesus, meaning Savior; because He would save people from their sins.

Over awed by the mystery of Mary having been chosen to be the mother of the Savior-King, Joseph's fears were banished. He did as the angel had commanded and married Mary as originally planned, but the marriage was not consummated until after the birth of her Son.

Joseph, of the lineage of David, was not the physical father of Jesus, but he became His legal father.

## Chapter Five

# Prophecies Concerning Messiah's Birthplace

### Bethlehem

> "But you, Bethlehem Ephrathah,
> Though you are little among
> the thousands of Judah,
> Yet out of you shall come forth to Me
> The One to be Ruler in Israel,
> Whose goings forth are from of old,
> From everlasting."
>
> Micah 5:2

### Fulfillment

Mary and Joseph were living in Nazareth prior to the birth of Jesus. And about that time, Caesar Augustus had ordered a census to be taken throughout the Roman Empire. In Israel, it was customary to register at a person's ancestral home, so Joseph and Mary traveled to Bethlehem, the city of David.

## Chapter 5

While they were there, the time came for Jesus to be born. However, as Bethlehem was crowded with visitors registering for the census, there were no rooms available. So Jesus was born in a humble stable, wrapped in strips of cloth, and laid in a manger.

### Witnesses: Angels

That night, shepherds were in the fields nearby guarding their sheep. When suddenly an angel appeared to them, and the light of God's glory shone around.

The angel told them not to be afraid, because he had some wonderful news for all people. That night the Savior, the Messiah and Ruler, had been born in David's town. He told the shepherds that they would find the Baby wrapped in pieces of cloth, and lying in a manger.

Then a huge angelic choir joined the first angel, singing God's praises and giving Him glory, announcing peace toward all men and women on earth.

### Witnesses: Shepherds

The shepherds quickly made their way to Bethlehem, and found Joseph and Mary, and the Baby lying in a manger. After the shepherds had seen Him, they spread the news of what had happened, and everyone who heard their story was amazed.

## Witness: Simeon

On the eight day, to fulfill the Jewish law, the Baby was circumcised and named Jesus. Then after Mary's days of purification were completed, they went to Jerusalem, to present their firstborn to God (Exodus 13:1-2; Leviticus 12:2-8; Luke 2:22-24).

Living in Jerusalem at that time was an old man named Simeon. He was a devout Jew, waiting expectantly for the coming of Israel's Messiah. It had been revealed to him by the Holy Spirit, that he would see the Messiah before he died. He was led by the Spirit to the Temple, just as Joseph and Mary arrived with Jesus to carry out the rituals of the Jewish law.

Simeon took Jesus up in his arms and blessed God. Then he said that the LORD could now let him depart in peace, for he had seen His salvation, a light of revelation to the Gentiles, and the glory of God's people, Israel.

## Witness: Anna The Prophetess

Anna was a widow and very old, and she continually served God in the Temple with fasting and prayers. Seeing Simeon holding Jesus, she also gave thanks to God for Him. Then she spoke about the Child to all who were waiting for national deliverance.

CHAPTER 5

## Witness: Three Learned Men

Sometime after Jesus was born, learned men came from the East to Jerusalem. They had seen a supernatural star announcing the birth of the King of the Jews, and had come to worship Him.

Herod was king at that time, and when he heard this news, he was deeply troubled. He gathered the Jewish religious scholars together to ask them where the Messiah would be born. They answered that it was written by the prophet Micah that the Messiah would be born in Bethlehem.

Then Herod held a secret meeting with the wise men to find out when the star had appeared. Then he sent them to Bethlehem, and told them to tell him when they found the Child. Herod was pretending that he also wanted to go and worship Him, but he intended to kill Him.

The star that the learned men had seen in the east went before them until it came to rest over the exact place where the Child was. When the three men entered the house and saw the Child with His mother, they fell down and worshiped Him. Then they presented Him with gifts of gold, frankincense, and myrrh.

The wise men were warned in a dream not to report back to Herod. So they returned to their own country by another route.

An angel warned Joseph in a dream that he must take the Child and His mother to Egypt because Herod would seek the Child to destroy Him. Joseph left while it was dark, taking Mary and Jesus with him. The family remained in Egypt until after Herod's death.

When Herod discovered that the wise men had deceived him, he flew into a rage. He gave orders for all the male children in Bethlehem, two years old and under, to be put to death, fulfilling Jeremiah's prophecy.

"A voice was heard in Ramah,

Lamentation and bitter weeping,

Rachel weeping for her children,

Refusing to be comforted for her children,

Because they are no more."

Jeremiah 31:15

## Chapter Six

# Prophecies of Messiah's Pre-Existence

### Everlasting Father, Prince of Peace

"But you, Bethlehem Ephrathah,

Though you are little

among the thousands of Judah,

Yet out of you shall come forth to Me

The One to be Ruler in Israel,

**Whose goings forth are from of old,**

**From everlasting.**"

                Micah 5:2, emphasis added

For unto us a Child is born,

Unto us a Son is given;

And the government will be upon

His shoulder.

And His name will be called

Wonderful, Counselor, Mighty God,

**Everlasting Father**, Prince of Peace.

Isaiah 9:6, emphasis added

The promised Saviour was both human and divine. He will reign forever on the throne of David, something that God Himself promises to accomplish.

## David's Lord

The LORD said to my Lord,

"Sit at My right hand,

Till I make Your enemies Your footstool."

Psalm 110:1; Matthew 22:44

David speaks of "my Lord," someone greater than himself, a reference to the coming Messiah. Jesus was a descendant of David, yet his pre-existent Lord.

Father God commands the Son to take His Kingdom back from His enemies. He also honors the Son with a priestly role forever, according to the order of Melchizedek, (Psalm 110:2-4; Hebrews 7:11-17).

CHAPTER 6

## John: The Eternal Word

> In the beginning was the Word, and the Word was with God, and the Word was God.     John 1:1

The apostle John begins his Gospel account with a bold and clear declaration of the deity of Jesus, and omits any reference to His human ancestry. John declares that all things were made through Him, and in Him was life. His light shone in the darkness. The Word became flesh and lived among us. His glory, the glory of the only begotten Son, was seen. He is full of grace and truth. (See John 1:3-5; 14.)

The divine and eternal Messiah existed before the earth and mankind were created. The LORD God's Anointed One preceded all written prophecies and any recorded genealogies.

## Chapter Seven

# Prophecies Concerning A Sacrificial Lamb

### THE LAMB OF GOD

> "**...God will provide for Himself the lamb for a burnt offering.**"
>
> Genesis 22:8, emphasis added

### Sin Entered The World

Adam and Eve sinned against God when they rebelled against His one commandment.

> And the LORD God commanded the man, saying, "Of every tree of the garden you may freely eat; but of the tree of the knowledge of good and evil you shall not eat, for in the day the you eat of it you shall surely die." Genesis 2:16-17

Sin and death entered humanity through their defiant disobedience, and mankind's nature became evil. Adam and Eve were then suddenly ashamed of their nakedness.

## Chapter 7

They covered themselves with fig leaves and hid from God's presence in shame and guilt.

## Sacrificial Redemption Prophesied

The serpent was cursed by God for instigating Adam and Eve's rebellion. God said there would be enmity between Satan's seed and the woman's Seed (Messiah), who will come and defeat Satan's followers. And Satan will "bruise" Messiah.

> He shall bruise your head,
>
> And you shall bruise His heel."
>
> Genesis 3:15b

> Yet it pleased the LORD to bruise Him;
>
> He has put Him to grief.
>
> When You make His soul an offering for sin,
>
> He shall see His seed, He shall
>
> prolong His days,
>
> And the pleasure of the LORD
>
> shall prosper in His hand.
>
> Isaiah 53:10

God did not excuse Eve's sin because she was deceived. He said that she would bear children in pain, and her husband would rule over her.

The ground was cursed because of Adam's sin, and he would experience hard labor in providing food from the fields. Then eventually he would die and return to the dust of the earth from which he was made.

## Sacrificial Blood

Yet God also showed Adam and Eve mercy. They had tried to cover their nakedness, but their self-efforts were inadequate. Before banishing them from the Garden of Eden, God made them clothing from animal skins, the first shedding of blood to provide covering.

## Cain And Abel

Time passed, and the two sons of Eve brought offerings to God. Cain was a farmer and brought some of the produce of his toil. Abel was a shepherd and, in faith, offered a sacrificed lamb, the firstborn of his flock. Abel's offering was accepted by God. But He did not respect Cain or his offering, and Cain was angry. Then God told Cain that there was no need to sulk. If he did well, he too would be accepted. But if he chose not to, sin was waiting to entice him. Ignoring God's advice and warning, Cain lured his brother into a field and murdered him.

## Fulfillment

Abel's sacrifice of a lamb made him righteous before God. Messiah, the Lamb of God, would be sacrificed to make sinners righteous, enabling them to have an intimate relationship with God and restoring what was lost by the sin in the Garden of Eden.

Chapter 7

## Abraham And Isaac

God commanded Abraham to take his son Isaac to the land of Moriah, about a three day journey. There, he was to offer Isaac as a burnt offering on one of the mountains that He would show him. So Abraham obeyed and went to the place God had told him.

Abraham told his servants to stay with the donkeys, while he and Isaac went to worship God. Then he made a remarkable statement of faith. He said that they would return. As God had promised to create a nation through Isaac, Abraham reasoned that even if he had to kill his son, God could bring him back to life.

Isaac carried the wood for the burnt offering, and Abraham carried the fire and the knife. As they set off together, Isaac asked his father where the lamb was for the sacrifice. And Abraham said that God Himself would provide the lamb for a burnt offering.

> **And Abraham said, "My son, God will provide for Himself the lamb for a burnt offering."** Genesis 22:8a

At the place God had appointed, Abraham built an altar and placed the wood on the top. Then he tied Isaac and laid him on the wood. Nothing is said in the biblical account concerning Isaac's reaction to this alarming turn of events. It would appear that he passively co-operated with his father's will, just as Jesus, at His appointed time, would surrender to God's will and allow Himself to be sacrificed.

> **He was led as a lamb to the slaughter,**
> **And as a sheep before its shearers is silent,**
> **So He opened not His mouth.**
>
> Isaiah 53:7b

As Abraham took his knife, the Angel of the LORD called his name and commanded him to stop. Then Abraham saw a ram caught in a bush by its horns, and he sacrificed it as a burnt offering.

Abraham had passed an extreme test of faith in not withholding his son, proving that he trusted God completely and would fully obey His commands. Therefore God promised to bless him and give him many descendants.

## Fulfillment

In this literal event, there was also a picture of a future event, when the Messiah, Son of God, would be sacrificed for the sins of all mankind. The atonement for sin was part of God's eternal plan. Jesus bore mankind's sins and was "cut off" from the land of the living. By His atoning death, any sinner who calls upon His name is justified and declared, "Not guilty."

The enemy of our souls would have delighted in the destruction of God's Son. But his celebration would not have lasted long, for on the third day, God's power would raise Jesus to life, in an eternal body.

Chapter 7

## Passover

> "Now the blood shall be a sign for you on the houses where you are. And when I see the blood, I will pass over you; and the plague shall not be on you to destroy you when I strike the land of Egypt."
>
> Exodus 12:13

Pharaoh had obstinately refused every command of God to release the Hebrews from slavery. As he continued to resist God, the series of plagues on Egypt became increasingly severe.

God sent Moses with a final warning for Pharaoh. Every firstborn of the people and animals in the land of Egypt would die, but all the children of Israel would be saved from this catastrophic disaster. Yet even then, Pharaoh would not relent.

God gave Moses instructions that would separate and preserve the children of Israel from His judgment. Every man must take a healthy male lamb for his family, and keep it until the fourteenth day of the first month. Then at twilight, the lamb was to be killed and some of its blood daubed on the doorposts and lintel of their house. The meat was to be roasted, and eaten with unleavened bread and bitter herbs. God's people were to eat this meal in a hurry, dressed ready to leave.

That night, God was going to pass through the land of Egypt and kill all the firstborn of both man and beast. He would also bring judgment on all the gods of Egypt. But when He saw the blood of the lamb on the houses, He would pass over, and the plague would not destroy them.

God ordained that this Passover feast was to be celebrated annually, and the story of His deliverance was to be faithfully related throughout the generations.

After the LORD had gone through the land and killed the firstborn, Pharaoh released God's people. And Moses led them out of Pharaoh's kingdom to serve the LORD God of Israel. Then Pharaoh regretted that he had released his former slaves, and his army pursued them to the Red Sea.

God's people were trapped between the Red Sea and the advancing Egyptian army. But God miraculously parted the waters, making a dry pathway through the sea. Having crossed safely to land on the other side, God brought the waters back together. So the Egyptians, with their horses and chariots, were drowned.

## Fulfillment

This actual event was also a picture of a future time, when the atoning blood of the Messiah, the Lamb of God, would save the sinner from God's judgment. And that sinner is freed from slavery, rescued from the kingdom of Satan, the slave master, and received as a free citizen into the Kingdom of the Living God.

When God took the Hebrews through the Red Sea, they were separated from their past associations, and were free to worship God. And when Believers in Jesus, the Lamb of God, are baptized, they figuratively "die" to their previous life, and are free to live as a new creation, belonging to God.

CHAPTER 7

## Forerunner Prophesy Fulfilled

John, the son of Zacharias, was in the wilderness until the appointed time for him to begin his ministry. When he finally burst onto the scene, prepared for his unique role and filled with the Holy Spirit, there was an excitement and fervent messianic expectancy among the Jews. Eager crowds flocked to hear John the Baptist's fearless and fiery messages of repentance, and many were baptized by him in the Jordan River.

The Jewish leaders sent priests and Levites from Jerusalem to question John about his identity. He told them that he was not the Messiah, or Elijah, or the prophet. (Moses had prophesied that a prophet would come like him, Deuteronomy 18:15).

Under further pressure to identify himself, John the Baptist claimed that he was the fulfillment of Isaiah's prophecy, saying:

> The voice of one crying in the wilderness:
> 
> "Prepare the way of the LORD;
> 
> Make straight in the desert
> 
> A highway for our God."
> 
> Isaiah 40:3; Matthew 3:3; John 1:23

When the Pharisees questioned his authority to baptize, John answered that he baptized with water. But there was One standing among them (John 1:26), mightier than him, who would baptize with the Holy Spirit and fire (Matthew 3:11; Luke 3:16; John 1:33).

## Witness: John The Baptist

> The next day John saw Jesus coming toward him, and said, "Behold! **The Lamb of God** who takes away the sin of the world! This is He of whom I said, 'After me comes a Man who is preferred before me, for **He was before me.**' "
> John 1:29-30, emphasis added

John witnessed to the identity of Jesus, and the purpose of His coming. He also witnessed to His pre-existence, saying that Jesus was greater than he, and that Jesus was before him. John was six months older than his cousin Jesus, yet stated that Jesus was before him.

When Jesus came to John to be baptized, God gave John a sign that Jesus was the Messiah, the Son of God. As he was baptizing Jesus, John witnessed this.

> ... Jesus came up immediately from the water; and behold, the heavens were opened to Him, and he saw the Spirit of God descending like a dove and alighting upon Him. And suddenly a voice came from heaven, saying, "This is My beloved Son, in whom I am well pleased."
> Matthew 3:16-17; Luke 3:21-22; John 1:32

CHAPTER 7

## Jesus' Test Before His Ministry

After His baptism, Jesus was led by the Spirit into the wilderness, to be tempted by the devil. He fasted for forty days and nights, and afterwards He was hungry. Then the Tempter came, saying that if He was the Son of God, He should turn the stones into bread.

> But He answered and said, "It is written, 'Man shall not live by bread alone, but by every word that proceeds from the mouth of God.' "
>
> Deuteronomy 8:3; Matthew 4:4
>
> Then the devil took Him up into the holy city, set Him on the pinnacle of the temple, and said to Him, "If You are the Son of God, throw Yourself down. For it is written: 'He shall give His angels charge over you,' and, 'In their hands they shall bear you up, Lest you dash your foot against a stone.' "
>
> Matthew 4:5; Psalm 91:11, 12
>
> Jesus said to him, "It is written again, 'You shall not tempt the LORD your God.' "
>
> Matthew 4:7; Deuteronomy 6:16

Then the devil took Jesus to the peak of a very high mountain, and showed Him all the kingdoms of the world. He said that he would give them all to Jesus if He would fall down and worship him.

> Then Jesus said to him, "Away with you, Satan! For it is written, 'You shall worship the LORD your God, and Him only you shall serve."
> 
> Matthew 4:10; Deuteronomy 6:13

With this, the devil left Jesus, and the angels came and took care of Him.

Adam had failed when tested, but Jesus triumphed over every temptation. And just as the lamb for the Passover feast had to be spotless, Jesus was undefiled by sin. He resisted and defeated Satan with the Word of God.

## Chapter Eight

# Prophecies of Messiah's Earthly Ministry

"The land of Zebulun

and the land of Naphtali,

By the way of the sea, beyond the Jordan,

Galilee of the Gentiles:

The people who sat in darkness

have seen a great light,

And upon those who sat in the

region and shadow of death

Light has dawned."

Matthew 4:15-16; Isaiah 9:1-2

## Fulfillment

Messiah entered this dark world to give spiritual light. John the Baptist was sent by God as a forerunner to testify of the Light, so that people might believe in Him and be saved. God promised Abraham that all families on earth would be blessed through him (Genesis 12:3),

In the land of Israel, from the lineage of Abraham, Isaac, and Jacob, the Messiah was born. He was destined to be a blessing to all nations on earth.

Jesus began His ministry in Galilee. He traveled through the region preaching repentance, teaching in the synagogues, and healing the people of all their sicknesses. News about Him spread throughout the surrounding regions and great crowds flocked to Him.

And it was from the region of Galilee that Jesus called His first disciples, Peter, Andrew, James, and John. They were fishermen, and Jesus promised to make Peter and Andrew a fisher of men (Matthew 4:18-19).

### Witness: Nathanael

When Nathanael heard from Philip about Jesus of Nazareth, he asked if anything good could come out of Nazareth. But when he met Jesus for the first time, Jesus already knew him. Astonished by Jesus' supernatural knowledge, Nathanael declared that He was the Son of God and the King of Israel!

## Isaiah

"The Spirit of the Lord GOD is upon Me,

Because the LORD has anointed Me

To preach good tidings to the poor;

## Chapter 8

> He has sent Me to heal the brokenhearted,
>
> To proclaim liberty to the captives,
>
> And the opening of the prison
>
> To those who are bound;
>
> **To proclaim**
>
> **the acceptable year of the LORD,"**
>
> Isaiah 61:1-2a, emphasis added

## Fulfillment

On a Sabbath day, Jesus read this portion of Scripture from Isaiah to the synagogue congregation in Nazareth. He told the people assembled there that this Scripture was now fulfilled. In applying these prophetic words to Himself, Jesus was claiming to be the Messiah, as well as declaring the purpose of His mission.

At first He was received well, but the congregation also remembered that he was only Joseph and Mary's son. And Jesus would not prove His claim by performing miraculous signs for them. He said that no prophet was welcome in his own town. Then He went on to say, that there had been many widows in Israel during three years of drought, but God did not send Elijah the prophet to any of them. He had only sent him to a widow in Zarephath in the region of Sidon.

And there were many lepers in Israel during the time of Elisha the prophet, but only Namaan the Syrian was cleansed. After hearing this, they were furious and dragged

Jesus to the edge of a cliff to throw Him over it. But Jesus calmly walked through the mob and went on His way! (See Luke 4:16-30.)

## Witnesses: John's Disciples

Now Herod Antipas had divorced his wife, in order to marry his niece. John the Baptist had publicly condemned him for this sin, and consequently Herod had ordered his arrest. (See Matthew 14:3.)

While in prison, John sent two of His disciples to Jesus, to ask whether He was the Coming One, or should they continue waiting? John's uncertainty is surprising, seeing that he had personally received a sign from God that Jesus was the Messiah. Possibly he had expectations of a conquering Messiah, as most Jews at that time were anticipating. Perhaps he had expected to be liberated from prison? But the Bible gives no explanation for his doubting.

Jesus told John's disciples to return to John and tell him the things they saw and heard Him doing. Captives were being released from sin, and there were miraculous healings. The blind could see, the lame could walk, and the deaf could hear! The Gospel was being preached to the poor. (See Luke 7:19-23.)

After John's disciples departed, Jesus praised John the Baptist, saying that he was a messenger from God, and a great prophet, and that it was written about him in the Scriptures, the one who would come and prepare the way for Messiah's coming (Matthew 11:10, Malachi 3:1).

CHAPTER 8

## Israel Rejects The Gospel

Jesus knew that He had a redemptive purpose to accomplish at His first coming, and had openly declared the predictions of His sufferings and death. But He said that He would be victorious over death, and spoke of His future glory. However, Jesus was misunderstood by the Jews when He said to them,

> "Destroy this temple, and in three days I will raise it up."        John 2:19

They thought He was speaking of the Temple building, but Jesus was speaking of the Temple of His body.

When the Jews pressed Him for a sign, Jesus spoke of Jonah, who was a sign of death and resurrection. Just as the prophet Jonah had been three days and three nights in the whale's belly, so He would be three days and three nights in the earth.

Jesus had also taught about the signs that would precede His second coming. But at that time, His disciples did not fully comprehend the things that he told them.

Knowing that the appointed time of His suffering was drawing near, Jesus was troubled. He said that when He was lifted up from the earth, He would draw all peoples to Himself, signifying the way He would die.

The crowd, knowing the Scriptures that spoke of the Messiah reigning triumphantly forever, questioned His statements. Even after all the miraculous signs and miracles they had witnessed, they did not believe in Him. Nevertheless, there were those who secretly believed, even among the leaders. But because of their fear of being put out of the Temple, they kept quiet.

## Prophecies of Messiah's Earthly Ministry

Six days before Passover, before His triumphal entry into Jerusalem and the confrontation in the Temple, Jesus stayed with His friends in nearby Bethany. While Jesus was eating with Lazarus, and Martha was serving, Mary took a very costly spikenard oil and anointed His feet. Then she wiped His feet with her hair. Judas Iscariot criticized her for wasting fragrant oil worth a year's wages, when it could have been sold and the money given to the poor.

> But Jesus said, "Let her alone; she has kept this for the day of My burial. For the poor you have with you always, but Me you do not have always."  John 12:7-8

Judas said what he did, not because he was concerned about the poor, but because he was a thief and used to steal from the disciples' money box.

## Prophecy, Entry Into Jerusalem As King

> "Rejoice greatly, O daughter of Zion!
>
> Shout, O daughter of Jerusalem!
>
> Behold, your King is coming to you;
>
> He is just and having salvation,
>
> Lowly and riding on a donkey,
>
> A colt, the foal of a donkey.
>
>                              Zechariah 9:9

CHAPTER 8

## Fulfillment

Jesus, knowing it would be His final journey, went up to Jerusalem with His disciples for the Passover feast. On this occasion He rode into the city on a donkey's colt, fulfilling Zechariah's prophecy and presenting Himself publicly as the Messiah and King of Israel.

## Witnesses: Disciples and Multitudes

As Jesus rode towards Jerusalem, large crowds accompanied Him. Some went before Him and cried out, saying:

> "Hosanna to the **Son of David!**
> 'Blessed is He who comes
> in the name of the LORD!'
> Hosanna in the highest!"
> Matthew 21:9; Psalm 118:26 emphasis added

When Jesus' procession entered Jerusalem, with the accompanying crowds loudly rejoicing and praising God, the whole city was shaken and wanted to know what was happening.

Jesus went straight to the Temple and drove out those who were buying and selling there. In righteous anger, He overturned the money changers' tables, and the seats of those selling doves.

> And He said to them, "It is written, 'My house shall be called a house of prayer,' but you have made it a 'den of thieves.' "
> Matthew 21:13; Isaiah 56:7

## Witnesses: The Lame, the Blind, and the Children

The blind and lame came to Jesus in the Temple and He healed them. But the chief priests and scribes were angered by Jesus' actions, and indignant when they heard the children shouting, "Hosanna to the Son of David!"

> **Jesus said to them, "Yes. Have you never read,' Out of the mouths of babes and nursing infants You have perfected praise'?"**
>
> **Matthew 21:16; Psalm 8:2**

The ordinary, and the disreputable people, had listened to John the Baptist's message of repentance and were baptized. But the religious leaders had refused to listen to John, or submit to being baptized by him. These same leaders also rejected and opposed Jesus. Throughout His ministry, they questioned His authority, and they looked for ways to outwit and trap Him.

Jesus had publicly accused these religious leaders of being outwardly pious, but secretly seeking prestige and power. He condemned them as being blind guides, neglecting justice, mercy, and truth. After Jesus' triumphal entry into Jerusalem as Messiah, they plotted together to kill Him. But not during the feast, for fear of the peoples' reaction.

Jesus, knowing the future events that would happen to Jerusalem and her people, wept with great compassion. He said that a time would come when enemies would destroy the city and not one stone of the Temple would

## Chapter 8

remain intact. They would not see Him again until they said,

> 'Blessed is He who comes in the name of the LORD!'"  Matthew 23:39

## Chapter Nine

# Prophecies of Messiah's Betrayal

## Betrayed By A Friend

> Even my own familiar friend
>
> in whom I trusted,
>
> Who ate my bread,
>
> Has lifted up his heel against me.
>
> Psalm 41:9; John 13:18

## Fulfillment

After Jesus's anointing at Bethany, Judas Iscariot went secretly to the chief priests. He asked what they would offer him to betray Jesus, and they gave him thirty pieces of silver (Matthew 26:14-16).

During the Passover meal with His disciples, Jesus was troubled. He said that one of them was going to betray Him. The disciples were stunned, and each of them began asking Him, "Lord, is it I?"

Jesus said that it was the disciple to whom he would give a piece of bread, after dipping it in the dish. Then He dipped the bread and gave it to Judas. After receiving the bread, Satan entered Judas and he immediately left the room. And it was night. (John 13:26-30)

## A New Covenant

> "Behold, the days are coming, says the LORD, when I will make a new covenant with the house of Israel and with the house of Judah—" Jeremiah 31:31

### Fulfillment

When God made a covenant with Abraham, concerning his descendants and the Land, blood sacrifices were made to confirm the binding agreement (Genesis 15). The sign of the covenant was circumcision (Genesis 17).

At the Passover meal, Jesus took the bread and broke it. Then he gave it to His disciples, saying that the bread was His body. He took the cup of wine, gave thanks and told them to drink from it. Jesus said,

> "For this is My blood of the new covenant, which is shed for many for the remission [forgiveness] of sins."
> Matthew 26:28, note added

## Forsaken By His Disciples

> "Awake, O sword, against My Shepherd,
>
> Against the Man who is My Companion,"
>
> Says the LORD of hosts.
>
> "Strike the Shepherd,
>
> And the sheep will be scattered;"
>
> Zechariah 13:7; Matthew 26:31

> "Indeed the hour is coming, yes, has now come, that you will be scattered, each to his own, and will leave Me alone. And yet I am not alone, because the Father is with Me." John 16:32

### Fulfillment

When Jesus told His disciples that they would all forsake Him as it was prophesied, Peter protested. He said that he would never deny Him. But Jesus answered, that the same night, before the rooster crowed, he would deny Him three times.

Then Jesus went out with His disciples to a place called Gethsemane. He told them to sit while He went a little further to pray. Deeply troubled, Jesus took Peter, James, and John with Him, and prayed to His Father. He asked if it were possible, for this cup of suffering to pass from Him. Nevertheless, not His will, but His Father's will be done.

## Chapter 9

As Jesus continued in anguished prayer, His three disciples fell asleep. And He warned them to be alert, His time of betrayal was near. While He was still speaking, Judas arrived with an armed crowd sent by the chief priests and elders of the people. He went straight to Jesus, and identified Him to the guards with a kiss. When they seized Jesus, Peter struck the high priest's servant with his sword and cut off his ear (John 18:10).

But Jesus told him to put his sword away, and He restored the man's ear. Jesus said that He had all heaven's power at His disposal, but it was His Father's will that the Scriptures concerning Him were fulfilled. At this point, all His disciples ran away

Jesus was arrested and led away to the high priest's house where the scribes and the elders had assembled. Peter followed at a distance, and then joined the servants and guards standing around the fire in the courtyard.

## Messiah Oppressed And Afflicted

> He was oppressed and He was afflicted,
> Yet He opened not His mouth;
> 
> Isaiah 53:7a

## Fulfillment

Throughout His unlawful arrest and trials, alone and undefended, Jesus acted with dignity. He remained silent as false witnesses accused Him.

Finally the high priest commanded Jesus, under oath by the living God, to say whether He was the Messiah, the

Son of God. Jesus answered in the affirmative. Then speaking prophetically of His second coming, He said to him,

> "It is as you said. Nevertheless, I say to you, hereafter you will see the Son of Man sitting at the right hand of the Power, and coming on the clouds of heaven."
>
> Matthew 26:64; Daniel 7:13

Jesus spoke truthfully, but the high priest accused Him of blasphemy, and all those assembled called for the death sentence. Then they began to spit in Jesus' face, and beat Him. Having blindfolded Him, they mockingly asked Jesus to prophesy who had struck Him.

Meanwhile, as Peter waited in the courtyard, a servant girl came to him and said that he was with Jesus of Galilee. But Peter denied it, and said that he didn't know what she was talking about. As he went out to the gateway, another girl also recognized him and said that he was with Jesus of Nazareth. But Peter swore that he did not know Him.

Later on, other bystanders insisted that Peter was one of the disciples, that it was obvious from his speech that he was a Galilean. Then Peter began to curse and swear, saying he did not know the Man. While he was still speaking, a rooster crowed. Then he remembered Jesus telling him that before the rooster crows, he would deny Him three times. Then Peter left the courtyard, weeping bitterly.

CHAPTER 9

## To Be Sold For Thirty Pieces Of Silver

> And the Lord said to me, "Throw it to the potter"—that princely price they set on me. So I took the thirty pieces of silver and threw them into the house of the Lord for the potter.
>
> Zechariah 11:13

### Fulfillment

Judas, seeing that Jesus was condemned, was overcome with remorse. He returned to the chief priests and the elders, saying that he had sinned in betraying innocent blood. But they were indifferent to his remorse. So he threw the silver pieces into the Temple, then went out and hanged himself (Matthew 27:3-5).

Knowing that it was unlawful to accept blood money as an offering in the Temple, they bought a potter's field, to bury strangers in. Therefore that field was known as the Field of Blood (Matthew 27:6-10).

## Chapter Ten

# Prophecies of Messiah's Suffering

### Lamb-Like

> He was led as a lamb to the slaughter,
> And as a sheep before its shearers is silent,
> So He opened not His mouth.
>
> Isaiah 53:7b

### Fulfillment

The Jewish leaders had no authority to execute Jesus, so the next morning He was taken to Pilate to be tried in the Roman Court.

Pilate asked Jesus if He was the King of the Jews, and Jesus answered that it was so. But during the incessant accusations of the chief priests and leaders, he remained silent. Pilate was astonished and impressed by Jesus, and he did not want to condemn Him. As it was customary for the Roman governor to release a prisoner during the Passover feast, Pilate wanted to release Jesus.

So he asked who they wanted him to set free, Barabbas, a notorious murderer and rebel against the Roman government, or Jesus, called Messiah. However, the chief

CHAPTER 10

priests and elders had already persuaded the gathered crowd to ask for the release of Barabbas. When Pilate asked what he should do with Jesus, they all said, "Let Him be crucified!" (Matthew 27:23).

When Pilate saw that he was getting nowhere in reasoning with the mob, and that a riot was imminent, he washed his hands in front of them, saying that he was innocent of the blood of this just Person. And all the people answered, "His blood be on us, and on our children" (Matthew 27:25). So Pilate reluctantly handed over Jesus to be scourged, a life threatening punishment.

## Messiah Disfigured beyond Recognition

> Behold, My Servant shall deal prudently;
> He shall be exalted and extolled
>   and be very high.
> Just as many were astonished at you,
> So His visage was marred
>   more than any man,
> And His form more than the sons of men;
>
> Isaiah 52:13-14

## Fulfillment

After Jesus was scourged, the Roman soldiers took Him to the Praetorium where the whole garrison gathered around Him. They dressed Him in a scarlet robe and pressed down a crown of thorns on His head. Then they placed a reed in His hand ,and knelt before Him in mock worship, saying, "Hail, King of the Jews!" (Matthew 27:29). They spat on Jesus, took the reed from His hand and beat Him on the head with it.

The brutal punishment of scourging and the subsequent abuse, disfigured His appearance until He was no longer recognizable. Having satisfied their sadistic pleasure, they took off the scarlet robe and returned His clothing. Then Jesus was led out to be crucified. The cruelest form of execution, reserved for the worst of criminals.

## Messiah was to be Pierced

> For dogs have surrounded Me;
> The congregation of the wicked
>   has enclosed Me.
> They pierced My hands and My feet;
>                          Psalm 22:16

This psalm of David's prophesies the crucifixion and suffering of Messiah, 1000 years before Jesus was physically born.

## Fulfillment

Exhausted and weakened, Jesus was unable to carry His cross. And one of the guards ordered a bystander, Simon of Cyrene, to carry Jesus' Cross to Golgotha.

Jesus was offered a mixture of wine and myrrh to dull His pain, but after tasting it, Jesus refused to drink. Then they nailed His hands and feet to the Cross.

CHAPTER 10

## They Gambled For Messiah's Garments

> They divide My garments among them,
>
> And for My clothing they cast lots.
>
> Psalm 22:18

## Fulfillment

The executioners had the right to take the victim's clothes. So after crucifying Jesus, the soldiers threw lots for His garments. Above Jesus' head there was a written sign.

THIS IS JESUS THE KING<br>OF THE JEWS.

## Messiah Crucified With Thieves

> And He was numbered
>
> with the transgressors,
>
> And He bore the sin of many,
>
> And made intercession
>
> for the transgressors.
>
> Isaiah 53:12b

## Fulfillment

Jesus was crucified with two robbers, one on either side of Him, and all those passing by contemptuously blasphemed Him. Jesus experienced cruel mockery and rejection, yet He responded with prayers for those who sinned against Him. He asked God the Father to forgive them because they were acting in ignorance.

## Messiah Is Despised And Rejected

> He is despised and rejected by men,
>
> A Man of sorrows and acquainted with grief.
>
> And we hid, as it were, our faces from Him;
>
> He was despised,
>
> and we did not esteem Him.
>
> Isaiah 53:3

> All those who see Me ridicule Me;
>
> They shoot out the lip,
>
> they shake the head, saying,
>
> "He trusted in the LORD,
>
> let Him rescue Him;
>
> Let Him deliver Him,
>
> since He delights in Him!"
>
> Psalm 22: 7-8

### Fulfillment

Those who passed by challenged Jesus to save Himself if He really was the Son of God! The religious leaders observed His suffering with indifference and joined in with the mockery. They said that He had saved others but could not save Himself. If He was the King of Israel, let Him come down from the cross! He trusted in God, claimed to be His Son, so let Him rescue Him!

## Messiah Is A Sin Offering

> But He was wounded for our transgressions,
>
> He was bruised for our iniquities;
>
> The chastisement for our peace
>
> was upon Him,
>
> And by His stripes we are healed.
>
> All we like sheep have gone astray;
>
> We have turned, every one, to his own way;
>
> And the LORD has laid on Him
>
> the iniquity of us all.
>
> Isaiah 53:5-6

## Fulfillment

Jesus' enemies continued to sneer, and even the two thieves next to Him joined in the insults and ridicule. What they did not comprehend, was that Jesus could have saved Himself, but He chose to endure His suffering, and remain on the Cross, in order that we be saved.

When arrested in the Garden of Gethsemane, Jesus had told Peter not to use force to defend Him. Didn't He realize that if He had chosen to ask His Father, He would have provided Him with more than twelve legions of angels? But then Scriptures would not have been fulfilled!

Jesus was willingly submitting to God's plan of salvation. He was going to fulfill what was written concerning Him in the Law of Moses, the Prophets, and the Psalms.

## Messiah Feels Forsaken By God

> My God, My God, why have You forsaken Me?    Psalm 22:1

## Fulfillment

From the sixth hour (noon), there was a supernatural darkness over all the land for three hours, and Jesus was hidden from the gaping crowd.

> About the ninth hour Jesus cried out with a loud voice, saying, "Eli, Eli, lama sabachthani?" that is, "My God, My God, why have You forsaken Me?"
> Matthew 27:46

Those words spoken by Jesus in Aramaic, were written by David 1000 years previously.

Hearing Jesus' cry of abandonment, some of the bystanders thought He was calling for Elijah. God was not turning from His Son, but from the sins His Son was bearing, at that time, for the whole world. Jesus had always been with the Father, and this must surely have caused Him to experience a most cruel sense of rejection and complete isolation.

Chapter 10

## Messiah Thirsts

> My strength is dried up like a potsherd,
>
> And My tongue clings to My jaws;
>
> You have brought Me to the dust of death.
>
> Psalm 22:15

> Reproach has broken my heart,
>
> And I am full of heaviness;
>
> I looked for someone to take pity,
>
> but there was none;
>
> And for comforters, but I found none.
>
> They also gave me gall for My food,
>
> And for my thirst
>
> they gave me vinegar to drink.
>
> Psalm 69:20-21

### Fulfillment

From the time of His arrest, until being crucified, Jesus had endured six separate trials and extremely brutal punishment. He suffered agonizing pain, exhaustion, and terrible thirst; as well as the emotional pain of scorn, rejection, and isolation.

One of those standing by the Cross ran and soaked a sponge with sour wine, then lifted it up on a stick for Him to drink. But others there told him not to bother. They wanted to see if Elijah would come and help Him.

## Chapter Eleven

# Prophecies of Messiah's Death and Burial

> Into Your hand I commit my spirit;
> Psalm 31:5

## Fulfillment

In spite of His physical weakness and thirst, Jesus cried out with a loud voice, "Father, 'into Your hands I commit My spirit' " (Luke 23:46).

Having accomplished God's redemption plan, and thereby finished His mission, Jesus yielded up His spirit to His Father.

## Witnesses: The Centurion and Soldiers

There was an earthquake, rocks were split, and many dead saints came back to life. When the centurion guarding Jesus saw what had happened, he glorified God, and said, "Certainly this was a righteous Man!" (Luke 23:47). And when the centurion, and those with him who were guarding Jesus, experienced the earthquake and the things that were happening, they said, "Truly this was the Son of God!" (Matthew 27:54).

## Witnesses: Many Women

There were many women who had followed Jesus, some from Galilee and others from Jerusalem. They stood at a distance watching these things. Among them were Mary Magdalene, Mary the mother of James and Joseph, and the mother of Zebedee's sons.

At the moment Jesus gave up His spirit, the veil in the Temple that separated the Holy Place from the Most Holy Place, was torn in two from top to bottom. The earth quaked, and rocks were split. Graves were opened and many bodies of saints were raised. (After Jesus' resurrection, these saints went into Jerusalem and appeared before many.)

In tearing the separating veil, God had made a direct and personal access to Himself through His Son's atoning death.

## Not One Of His Bones Broken

> In one house it (the Passover lamb)* shall be eaten; you shall not carry any of the flesh outside the house, nor shall you break one of its bones.
>
> Exodus 12:46, *author's note

It was the Preparation Day, and the bodies could not remain on the crosses during Sabbath. So the Jews asked Pilate to break their legs to hasten death, and their bodies taken away. So the soldiers broke the legs of the two criminals on either side of Jesus; but seeing that Jesus was already dead, they did not break His legs.

## Messiah's Side Is Pierced

"And I will pour on the house of David and on the inhabitants of Jerusalem the Spirit of grace and supplication; then they will look on Me whom they pierced.

*Zechariah 12:10a*

## Fulfillment

One of the soldiers pierced Jesus' side with a spear, and blood and water came out (John 19:34).

## Buried With The Rich

And they made His grave with the wicked—

But with the rich at His death,

Because He had done no violence,

Nor was any deceit in His mouth.

*Isaiah 53:9*

## Fulfillment

It was the Roman custom to throw crucified bodies to the dogs. But Joseph of Arimathea, a rich man and a secret disciple of Jesus, asked Pilate for the body of Jesus. Pilate gave his permission, and Joseph took the body away.

Chapter 11

# Witnesses: Joseph of Arimathea and Nicodemus

Then Nicodemus, who was also a secret disciple, came openly with myrrh and aloes. They covered Jesus' body with the spices and bound Him with clean linen cloths. Then they placed His body into Joseph's tomb, which had been recently cut out of the rock. Afterwards, they rolled a large stone across the entrance of the tomb.

On the Day of Preparation, the Jewish leaders went to Pilate and told him that Jesus had claimed He would arise from the dead after three days. Therefore they asked for the tomb to be guarded until the third day; otherwise, His disciples might steal the body and deceive the people, saying that Jesus had risen from the dead.

Pilate agreed to their request and told them to go and secure the tomb. So they sealed the stone across the entrance and put soldiers there to guard it.

## Chapter Twelve

# Prophecies of Messiah's Resurrection

## Power Over Death

> For You will not leave my soul in Sheol,
>
> Nor will You allow
>
> Your Holy One to see corruption.
>
> Psalm 16:10

## Fulfillment

Early in the morning, on the first day of the week, Mary Magdalene and the other Mary came to the tomb. Suddenly there was an earthquake and an angel of God descended from heaven.

He rolled away the stone from the entrance of the tomb and sat on it. Shafts of light shone from him, and his garments were white as snow. The soldiers guarding the tomb were so afraid, they could not move!

The angel told the women not to be afraid. Jesus was not there. He had risen, just as He had promised. The angel invited them to look into the empty tomb where Jesus had been laid. Then he told them to go quickly and

## Chapter 12

tell the disciples that Jesus had risen and was going on ahead of them to Galilee.

## Witnesses: Soldiers, The Two Women, and The Disciples

Full of wonder, the women left the tomb and ran to tell the disciples. As they were going, Jesus met them, saying, "Rejoice!" So they fell to their knees, embracing His feet and worshiping Him (Matthew 28:9).

Meanwhile, some of the guards returned to the city and told the high priests everything that had happened. Then the priests gathered the elders together and came up with a plan. They bribed the soldiers with a large sum of money to say that Jesus's disciples had come at night and stolen His body while they were sleeping (Matthew 28:11-15).

That evening, the disciples gathered together in a locked room because they were afraid of the Jews. Suddenly Jesus stood among them and said, "Peace be with you." (John 20:19) Then he showed them His hands and His pierced side.

> **So Jesus said to them again, "Peace to you! As the Father has sent Me, I also send you." And when He had said this, He breathed on them, and said to them, "Receive the Holy Spirit." John 20:21-22**

Now Thomas was absent at that time, and the other disciples told him they had seen the Lord. But he said that unless he saw and touched Jesus' wounds, he would not believe.

PROPHECIES OF MESSIAH'S RESURRECTION

After eight days, Jesus came again to His disciples. He told Thomas to see and touch His wounds, and to stop being unbelieving,

> And Thomas answered and said to Him, "My Lord and my God!" Jesus said to him, "Thomas, because you have seen Me, you have believed. Blessed are those who have not seen and yet have believe."
>
> John 20:28-29

## Witnesses: Over 500 people

In the early morning, Jesus had appeared to Mary Magdalene, and the other Mary. Then during the afternoon, He appeared to two of His disciples on the way to Emmaus (Mark 16:3, Luke 23:13-32). That evening He appeared to ten of His disciples, and eight days later to His eleven disciples, including Thomas.

Sometime later He appeared to seven of His disciples in Galilee, and all of His disciples saw Him at His Ascension (John 21; Acts 1:11).

The apostle Paul recorded that Jesus was seen by Peter, then by the other disciples. After that He was seen by more than five hundred brethren at once. Afterwards He was seen by James. Last of all, Paul himself experienced an encounter with the Risen Lord, and heard His voice. (1 Corinthians 15:5-8; Acts 9:3-6)

CHAPTER 12

## Victorious Over Death

> He will swallow up death forever,
>
> And the Lord God will wipe away
>
> tears from all faces;
>
> The rebuke of His people
>
> He will take away from all the earth;
>
> For the LORD has spoken.
>
> Isaiah 25:8

> "For as Jonah was three days and nights in the belly of the great fish, so will the Son of Man be three days and three nights in the heart of the earth." Matthew 12:40

Elisha the prophet brought a child back to life. Then when the body of a dead man was thrown on Elisha's grave, immediately when it touched the prophet's bones, the man was restored to life (2 Kings 4:34-35; 2 Kings 13:20-21).

During Jesus' ministry, He raised Lazarus from the dead, and many Jews believed in Him because of this miracle.

> Jesus said to her, "I am the resurrection and the life. He who believes in Me, though he may die, he shall live. And whoever lives and believes in Me shall never die. Do you believe this?" John 11:25-26

## Prophecies of Messiah's Resurrection

Although many references to faith in the resurrection of the dead are recorded in the Bible, the Sadducees denied this belief and taught solely from the five books of Moses.

And one day, while Jesus was teaching in the Temple, the Sadducees asked Him a question concerning the resurrection and Jewish marriage customs. Jesus replied that those who were included in the resurrection would not marry. They would be like the angels of God.

He also pointed out that Moses, in recording God's words to him from the burning bush, had clearly shown that the dead are raised to life,

> Moreover He said, "I am the God of your father — the God of Abraham, the God of Isaac, and the God of Jacob." And Moses hid his face, for he was afraid to look upon God.   Exodus 3:6

> "But concerning the resurrection of the dead, have you not read what was spoken to you by God, saying, 'I am the God of Abraham, the God of Isaac, and the God of Jacob'? God is not the God of the dead, but of the living."   Matthew 22:31-32

### Fulfillment

During the forty days from His victory over the grave to the day He was taken up to heaven, Jesus' disciples walked, talked, and ate with the Risen Lord. Having fulfilled many of the Biblical prophecies, Jesus opened up their minds to understand all that the prophets had written about Him.

Jesus' glorified body had visible marks of the nails in His hands and feet, and of the wound in His side. But in the power of His glorified body, Jesus was no longer subject to the physical sufferings and limitations of human life.

## Messiah Is Our Saviour

> And it shall come to pass
>
> That whoever calls
>
> on the name of the LORD
>
> Shall be saved.
>
> Joel 2:32; Romans 10:11-13

During Jesus' time on earth, He was entirely dedicated to His Father's will. Jesus is the sinless, sacrificial Lamb of God. His death and shed blood secured a perfect salvation for all those who would repent and believe in Him.

> "For the life of the flesh is in the blood, and I have given it to you upon the altar to make atonement for your souls; for it is the blood that makes atonement for the soul." Leviticus 17:11

> "For God so loved the world that He gave His only begotten Son, that whoever believes in Him should not perish but have everlasting life." John 3:16

## Chapter Thirteen

# Prophecies of Messiah's Second Coming

## Messiah's Return Promised

"I was watching in the night visions,
And behold, One like the Son of Man,
Coming with the clouds of heaven!
He came to the Ancient of Days,
And they brought Him near before Him."

Daniel 7:13

"Men of Galilee, why do you stand gazing up into heaven? This same Jesus, who was taken up from you into heaven, will so come in like manner as you saw Him go into heaven." Acts 1:11

## Chapter 13

> Behold, He is coming with clouds, and every eye will see Him, even they who pierced Him. And all the tribes of the earth will mourn because of Him. Even so, Amen.  Revelation 1:7

At the end of His earthly ministry, Jesus met with His disciples on the Mount of Olives and instructed them to wait in Jerusalem for the outpouring and baptism of the Holy Spirit, which would empower them to witness.

His disciples were eager to know when Jesus would restore the kingdom to Israel. But Jesus said that it was not for them to know the times set by His Father. After saying these things, He blessed His disciples, and while they were watching, Jesus was taken up to heaven in a cloud.

While His disciples were watching His ascent, two angels appeared to them, and they promised that Jesus would return in the same way that they had seen Him leave.

Enoch did not experience death, his body was caught up to God while he was living. And while Elijah the prophet was still alive, he was taken up to heaven by angels. Enoch and Elijah ascended as servants of God. But Messiah arose from the dead, and in a glorified body He ascended to heaven, as the Son of God.

Messiah's second coming will be at a time when the Anti-Christ has already appeared on the political scene. As this charismatic and manipulative leader rises to dominant world power, he will make a treaty with Israel and gain favor with the Jewish people.

Half way through his allotted time to rule, Anti-Christ's deception and treachery will be revealed when he demands to be worshiped as God. The Jews will refuse to obey this blasphemous command and Anti-Christ will turn against them. He will incite war against the nation of Israel, and provoke worldwide persecution against Jews (Daniel 9:27; 11:36).

## All Nations Gather Against Israel

> "And it shall happen in that day that I will make Jerusalem a very heavy stone for all peoples; all who would heave it away will surely be cut in pieces, though all nations of the earth are gathered against it."
>
> Zechariah 12:3

This universal attack will be disastrous for Israel, as two out of every three Jews will be killed. However, a third are saved by God's merciful intervention.

Jeremiah spoke of these future events. "Alas! For that day is great, so that none is like it; and it is the time of Jacob's trouble, but he shall be saved out of it" (Jeremiah 30:7).

And Daniel also prophesied concerning this period, "At that time Michael shall stand up, the great prince who stands watch over the sons of your people; and there shall be a time of trouble, such as never was since there was a nation, even to that time. And at that time your people shall be delivered, everyone who is found written in the book" (Daniel 12:1).

Chapter 13

# God's Day of Vengeance

> "To proclaim
>
> the acceptable year of the LORD,
>
> And the day of vengeance of our God;"
>
> Isaiah 61:2

At the beginning of Jesus' public ministry, full of the Holy Spirit, He returned to Galilee and taught in the synagogues. When He went into the synagogue in Nazareth on the Sabbath day and stood up to read, He was handed the scroll of the prophet Isaiah.

Reading from the beginning of chapter 61, Jesus declared the following words: "The Spirit of the Lord GOD is upon Me, because the LORD has anointed Me to preach good tidings to the poor; He has sent Me to heal the brokenhearted, to proclaim liberty to the captives, and the opening of the prison to those who are bound; to proclaim the acceptable year of the LORD,..." (Isaiah 61:1-2).

Then He stopped in the middle of the sentence, and sat down. He did not continue reading because He was the fulfillment of those prophetic words, the long awaited Messiah. The time of God's mercy and favor had come to Israel.

The next part of the sentence refers to the day of God's vengeance and will be fulfilled at the time of Messiah's second coming.

PROPHECIES OF MESSIAH'S SECOND COMING

## The Day Of The Lord

> Then the LORD will go forth
> And fight against those nations,
> As He fights in the day of battle.
> And in that day His feet will stand
>   on the Mount of Olives,
> Which faces Jerusalem on the east.
> And the Mount of Olives
>   shall be split in two,
> From east to west,
> Making a very large valley;
> Half of the mountain shall move
>   toward the north
> And half of it toward the south.
> Then you shall flee through
>   My mountain valley,
> For the mountain valley
>   shall reach to Azal.
> Yes, you shall flee
> As you fled from the earthquake
> In the days of Uzziah king of Judah.
> 
>                     Zechariah 14:3-5

## Chapter 13

When God judged Egypt with series of plagues, Pharaoh was forced to release God's people. Then after Moses had led them out of Egypt, Pharaoh changed his mind, and the Egyptian army pursued his former slaves.

By this time, as we noted earlier, the Hebrews were camping at the Red Sea. So they were trapped between the advancing army and the Sea. There was nowhere to flee, but God Himself intervened. He miraculously parted the waters, making a way of escape for His people.

He also destroyed the Egyptians that had pursued them into the sea, by bringing the waters back together and drowning them (Exodus 15:3-5).

In like manner, at a future time, when Israel has lost all hope of survival, God Himself will intervene. He will provide a way of escape. And He will also bring His judgment on the nations attacking them, with a supernatural plague on their bodies and minds. Then in their confusion, they will fight against each other (Zechariah 14:!2-13).

## Spirit Of Grace And Supplication

> "And I will pour on the house of David and on the inhabitants of Jerusalem the Spirit of grace and supplication; then they will look on Me whom they pierced. Yes, they will mourn for Him as one mourns for his only son, and grieve for Him as one grieves for a firstborn."  Zechariah 12:10

At this time He will show mercy on the remnant of Israel and the Holy Spirit will bring revelation to their hearts and minds. They will know that the One they rejected and killed, is the Messiah. As a result, there will be deep repentance, and they will mourn bitterly.

## Spiritual Cleansing And Renewal

> "In that day a fountain shall be opened for the house of David and for the inhabitants of Jerusalem, for sin and for uncleanness."
> Zechariah 13:1

There will also be a future spiritual cleansing of the land. All forms of idolatry will be banished and any false prophet who continues to practice these things will be put to death (Deuteronomy 18:20). Purged and refined, Jerusalem will emerge as the holy city of God.

## Messiah Descends onto the Mount of Olives

> Then the LORD will go forth
> And fight against those nations,
> As He fights in the day of battle.
> And in that day His feet will stand
>   on the Mount of Olives,
> Zechariah 14:3-4a

> Thus the LORD my God will come, and all the saints with You.       Zechariah 14:5b

Chapter 13

Messiah will descend onto the Mount of Olives with resurrected believers, and His coming will cause momentous geological changes. There will be an earthquake. The Mount of Olives will split in two, making a valley through which the besieged remnant can escape. Jerusalem will be raised up and leveled off, becoming the highest mountain in that area. This is an event foretold by both Isaiah and Micah (Isaiah 2:2; Micah 4:1).

## Cosmic Upheaval

> It shall come to pass in that day that there will be no light; the lights will diminish.
>
> Zechariah 14:6

Before the glorious reign of Messiah, there will be cosmic upheavals and dark days of judgment; a time like no other in earth's history (Joel 2:10-11; Malachi 3:2-3).

## God, The Glory Of His People

> "The sun shall no longer
>   be your light by day,
> Nor for brightness
>   shall the moon give light to you;
> But the LORD will be to you
>   an everlasting light,
> And your God your glory."
>
> Isaiah 60:19

In that day, as a result of the geological changes, fountains will burst forth. Jerusalem will become a source of living water, flowing into two rivers. One river will flow towards the Dead Sea, and the other to the Mediterranean Sea, They will irrigate the land in both summer and winter. Ezekiel prophesied that these living waters would bring life and healing wherever they flowed, (Ezekiel 47:9).

## Resurrection

"And He will send His angels with a great sound of a trumpet, and they will gather together His elect [chosen ones] from the four winds, from one end of heaven to the other." Mathew 24:31; 1 Corinthians 15:52

## Judgment

"The Son of Man will send out His angels, and they will gather out of His kingdom all things that offend, and those who practice lawlessness, and will cast them into the furnace of fire. There will be wailing and gnashing of teeth." Matthew 13:41-42

## Justice

"Then the righteous will shine forth as the sun in the kingdom of their Father. He who has ears to hear, let him hear!"
Matthew 13:43

## Chapter Fourteen

# Prophecies of Messiah's Everlasting Kingdom

"Yet I have set My King on My holy hill of Zion."                     Psalm 2:6

Then to Him was given dominion and glory and a kingdom, that all peoples, nations, and languages should serve Him.

His dominion is an everlasting dominion, which shall not pass away,

And His kingdom the one which shall not be destroyed.             Daniel 7:14

And the LORD shall be

King over all the earth.

In that day it shall be —

"The LORD is one," and His name one.

                              Zechariah 14:9

King David prophesied that Messiah would reign as King from the throne of David in Jerusalem, and that all those who rebelled against Him would perish. Daniel prophesied that Messiah's Kingdom would be an everlasting Kingdom, and that He will exercise absolute rule over all the nations. And Zechariah prophesied that a day would come when Messiah would be King over all the earth.

## Messiah the Righteous King

"Behold, the days are coming,"

says the LORD,

"That I will raise to David a

Branch of righteousness;

A King shall reign and prosper,

And execute judgment

and righteousness in the earth."

Jeremiah 23:5

And it shall come to pass that everyone who is left of all the nations which came against Jerusalem shall go up from year to year to worship the King, the LORD of hosts, and to keep the Feast of Tabernacles.

Zechariah 14:16

## Chapter 14

Messiah will judge the nations with perfect righteousness. Repentant and believing people among those nations that attacked Jerusalem will worship the King and celebrate the Feast of Tabernacles. Those who are unwilling to worship the King, and attend the yearly thanksgiving feast will experience God's wrath (Micah 4:2).

During Messiah's reign, the people of Judah and Jerusalem will fulfill their destiny as a holy priesthood belonging to God.

> "Remember the former things of old,
>
> For I am God, and there is no other;
>
> I am God, and there is none like Me,
>
> Declaring the end from the beginning,
>
> And from ancient times
>
>   things that are not yet done,
>
> Saying, 'My counsel shall stand,
>
> And I will do all My pleasure.' "
>
> Isaiah 46:9-10

In the beginning was the Word
And the Word was God.
When He created you and me
in His image,
He created us in love.
We were created for His pleasure,
To love Him and each other.
His peace surround you,
His love uphold you,
Shalom, Shalom.

Pauline Shone

## About the Author

After studying at The Central School of Art and Wimbledon School of Art in London, Pauline Shone gained a degree in Art and Design and began her working life as an Art teacher. Then a commission from Spode China, propelled her into a career as a freelance designer and sculptor for the ceramic industry in Stoke-on-Trent, England, a city often referred to as "The Potteries." Over the following twenty years Pauline's sculptures were manufactured by several china factories; however she is mainly known for her extensive range of sculptures produced for Spode China Ltd.

Although Pauline had a successful career, she was inwardly unfulfilled and searching for a deeper meaning to life. At the age of forty, while reading *Appointment in Jerusalem*, Lydia Prince's personal testimony, Pauline understood that Jesus was alive and actively involved in people's lives. Soon after this personal revelation, she was baptized in water and a few months later was baptized in the Holy Spirit.

Then Pauline's successful career came to an unexpected and abrupt end. This led to a difficult period, during which her priorities dramatically changed. Pauline then attended Torchbearers Bible College in Lancashire and later became involved with missions.

During her time working in Haifa, Israel, Pauline taught English at Beit Nitzachon Drug and Alcohol Rehabilitation Center. She also helped in two of HaCarmel Congregation's other ministries: Raven's Basket (a practical outreach to the poor, both Jews and Arabs) and Elijah's cave (intercession).

In her free personal time, Pauline was also using her creativity and experience of producing original prototypes for reproduction to write and illustrate Children's Bible Stories. In 2000, while she was working in Israel, the first seven books were accepted for publication by Authentic Media, India.

Shortly afterwards Pauline returned to England and devoted her time solely to writing and art work. She has returned to Israel several times since, including twice for three-month volunteer periods with Bridges for Peace and Succat Hallel, both based in Jerusalem.

Pauline produced 16 children's books, and over the years more than 400,000 copies have been sold in Asia. Then Pauline produced two illustrated booklets for teens based on the Bible characters, Ruth and Queen Esther, now republished as one book. Most of her other books have been republished. See pages 98 and 99.

In 2014, *Lamb of God, Key Messianic Prophecies,* was her first book for adults, now being republished. Her second book for adults, *Israel and the Nations,* published in 2017, is a further development of the same theme. Pauline is presently researching material for another book.

Pauline lives in England. She has a son, a daughter, four grandchildren, and a great grandson.

# Other Books by the Author

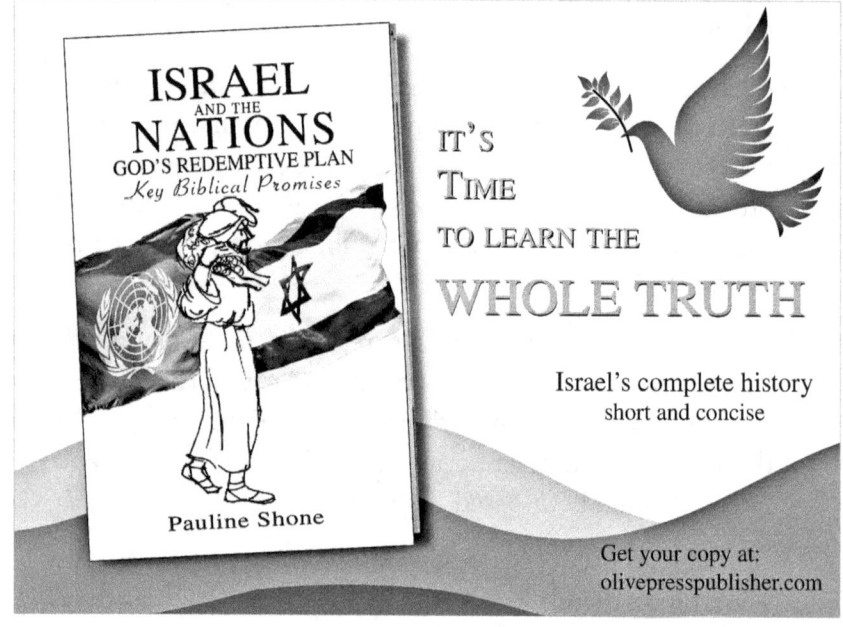

ISRAEL AND THE NATIONS *God's Redemptive Plan*
is Pauline's follow up book to this *LAMB OF GOD* book.

OlivePressBooks.com

OlivePressPublisher.com

***ISRAEL AND THE NATIONS*** *God's Redemptive Plan,* through Pauline's non-political, non-emotionally-charged, research-based approach, skillfully and concisely gives us the big historical picture of the Jewish relationship to God and The Land—from Abraham to 2017—along with spiritual insights. Even if you know Israel's Biblical history, do you know what happened to The Land during the first few centuries A.D. and during Medieval times? Become informed about this historical and spiritual account that is very pertinent to current events.

## ENDORSEMENTS

In a time where claims and counter-claims about Israel/Palestine have become narratives set adrift from fact, this work of Pauline Shone's is a refreshing change. Usually we are confronted, from both sides of this wrenching dispute, with fragmentary data and strident claims. Elegantly concise and workmanlike, *Israel and the Nations* tells the essentials of the entire Biblical/historical record. It is a dispassionate retelling of the Jewish people's relationship to The Land. For the person first coming to the topic it is a fine introduction to the long, historical sweep of this issue. For those familiar with the issues, it is an excellent reminder of the consistent Biblical and spiritual roots of the Jewish people's place in The Land.

**The Rev. Cn. Daryl Fenton**
**Director (CEO), CMJ Israel**

I warmly recommend this book to those seeking to learn about the history of the Jewish people, and God's plans and purposes for them. It is a useful educational and inspirational resource, well written, informative and concise.

**Sharon Sanders**
**Co-Founder and Director of the Ministry of Teaching**
**Christian Friends of Israel, Jerusalem**

# Children's Books by the Author

## Feed My Lambs series, colouring books
### 8.5 x 11 for children ages 3-7

## Feed My Sheep series for children ages 8-12
### Illustrated Bible stories 8.5 x 11

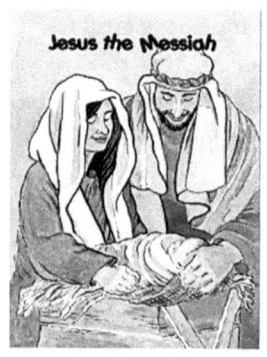

## Illustrated Bible story books 6x9

## Bible story in full colour hard cover 8x10

## Bible study book for teens 6x9

www.ingramcontent.com/pod-product-compliance
Lightning Source LLC
Chambersburg PA
CBHW051954290426
44110CB00015B/2237